C000185390

GRANDAD'S
WIT AND WISDOM
QUIPS AND QUOTES FOR GLORIOUS GRANDPAS

RICHARD BENSON

summersdale

GRANDAD'S WIT AND WISDOM

Research by Katherine Kingsford

Summersdale Publishers Ltd
46 West Street
Chichester
West Sussex
PO19 1RP
UK

www.summersdale.com

Printed and bound in the Czech Republic

ISBN: 978-1-78685-062-1

Substantial discounts on bulk quantities of Summersdale books are available to corporations, professional associations and other organisations. For details contact general enquiries: telephone: +44 (0) 1243 771107, fax: +44 (0) 1243 786300 or email: enquiries@summersdale.com.

CONTENTS

EDITOR'S NOTE

My uncle called his grandfather 'Go-go' when he was little because as a baby he could not pronounce the word 'Grandad'. When he got older and thought that sounded too childish, he changed it to 'Goeg'. My own grandfather was often known as 'Toppy'. I even know two girls who call their grandad 'Oompa'. I've heard Pop, Gaffer, Grumpy, Gramps and Tad-cu. It doesn't matter what name you use, the words mean the same. The father of your parent. Bigger than them; and, of course, anything greater is Grand. So there he is – the Grandfather. The great head of the family. The Patriarch.

Of course, all families are different. All families are a little crazy. But if family is the most important thing there is, those of us lucky enough to know the generations before our own should venerate and treasure them.

So it doesn't matter if he's known as Grandad or Taid. It doesn't matter whether you'll find him in the greenhouse or the pub. It doesn't matter whether he wears a flat cap or a silk cravat. What matters is that we realise how lucky we are to have his wisdom, his advice, his experience. For he is wonderful. He is grand. And, Grandad, we love you.

WHAT IS A GRAND-FATHER?

The simplest toy, one which
even the youngest child can
operate, is called a grandparent.

SAM LEVENSON

The perfect granddad is unafraid
of big dogs and fierce storms but
absolutely terrified of the word 'Boo'.

ROBERT BRAULT

Nobody can do for little children
what grandparents do. Grandparents
sort of sprinkle stardust over
the lives of little children.

ALEX HALEY

A GRANDFATHER SHARES HIS WISDOM, HIS STORIES, AND MOST IMPORTANTLY A LOVE THAT IS DIFFERENT FROM ALL OTHER LOVES.

Catherine Pulsifer

There is no greater achievement than being a grandfather who tells fairy tales to grandchildren.

ERALDO BANOVAC

Surely, two of the most satisfying experiences in life must be those of being a grandchild or a grandparent.

DONALD A. NORBERG

If I had known how wonderful it would be to have grandchildren, I'd have had them first.

LOIS WYSE

Being grandparents sufficiently removes us from the responsibilities so that we can be friends.

ALLAN FROME

This is a grandchild's ultimate privilege: knowing that someone is on your side, always.

FREDRIK BACKMAN

My grandkids believe I'm the oldest thing in the world… after two or three hours with them, I believe it, too.

GENE PERRET

SOMETHING MAGICAL HAPPENS WHEN PARENTS TURN INTO GRANDPARENTS.

Paul Linden

Just as a father feels it is all ending... in midlife, Dad may experience his second 'fatherhood' as a grandparent.

ALVIN FRANCIS POUSSAINT

IT IS INTO US THAT THE LIVES OF GRANDPARENTS HAVE GONE.

Charles and Ann Morse

The world becomes a more vulnerable place when one has a grandchild.

C. K. WILLIAMS

The only people interested in hearing about your grandchildren are other grandparents who want to tell you about theirs.

BRYNA NELSON PASTON

The reason grandchildren and grandparents get along so well is that they have a common enemy.

SAM LEVENSON

You start to act all goofy
and do things you never thought
you'd do. It's terrific.

MIKE KRZYZEWSKI ON BECOMING A GRANDPARENT

GRANDCHILDREN ARE GOD'S WAY OF COMPENSATING US FOR GROWING OLD.

Mary H. Waldrip

THE GRANDCHILD COMETH!

Children's children are a
crown to the aged.

PROVERBS 17:6

One of the most powerful handclasps
is that of a new grandbaby around
the finger of a grandfather.

JOY HARGROVE

Ah, babies! They're more than
just adorable little creatures on
whom you can blame your farts.

TINA FEY

Every baby needs a lap.

Henry Robin

A baby boy has a special
way of bringing out… the little
boy in his grandfather.

TANYA MASSE

BABIES ARE ALWAYS MORE
TROUBLE THAN YOU THOUGHT —
AND MORE WONDERFUL.

Charles Osgood

Children will not remember
you for the material things you
provided but for the feeling that
you cherished them.

RICHARD L. EVANS

Bring very old and very young
together: they interest one another.

JOHN CAGE

[A baby is] a loud noise at
one end and no sense of
responsibility at the other.

RONALD KNOX

The best baby-sitters, of course,
are the baby's grandparents…
which is why most grandparents
flee to Florida.

DAVE BARRY

Babies used to make me nervous, but
these squirmy things are awesome
once you've read the manual.

DAVID Z. HIRSCH

Babies laughing is like opium.

NEIL PATRICK HARRIS

Getting down on all fours
and imitating a rhinoceros
stops babies from crying.

P. J. O'ROURKE

EVERY BABY BORN INTO THE WORLD
IS A FINER ONE THAN THE LAST.

Charles Dickens

A child is a curly, dimpled lunatic.
RALPH WALDO EMERSON

Every child begins the world again.
HENRY DAVID THOREAU

Life is a flame that is always burning
itself out, but… catches fire again
every time a child is born.
GEORGE BERNARD SHAW

FAMILY
MATTERS!

Family is the most important
thing in the world.

DIANA, PRINCESS OF WALES

The only rock I know that stays
steady, the only institution I
know that works, is the family.

LEE IACOCCA

Your sons weren't made to like you.
That's what grandchildren are for.

JANE SMILEY

LOVE IS THE GREATEST GIFT THAT ONE GENERATION CAN LEAVE TO ANOTHER.

Richard Garnett

Setting a good example for your
children takes all the fun out
of middle age.

WILLIAM FEATHER

Never judge someone
by their relatives.

CHARLES MARTIN

To love at all is to be vulnerable.

C. S. LEWIS

Home is the one place in all this world where hearts are sure of each other.
FREDERICK W. ROBERTSON

Some family trees bear an enormous crop of nuts.
WAYNE HUIZENGA

If the family were a fruit, it would be an orange, a circle of sections, held together but separable.
LETTY COTTIN POGREBIN

IN TIME OF TEST,
FAMILY IS BEST.

Burmese proverb

Every human being who loves
another loves imperfection, for there
is no perfect being on this earth.

SUSAN COOPER

Our ancestors dwell in the
attics of our brains.

SHIRLEY ABBOTT

Posterity is the patriotic
name for grandchildren.

ART LINKLETTER

Other things may change us, but
we start and end with family.

ANTHONY BRANDT

Family – that dear octopus from
whose tentacles we never quite
escape, nor, in our inmost hearts,
ever quite wish to.

DODIE SMITH

The happiness of the domestic
fireside is the first boon of Heaven.

THOMAS JEFFERSON

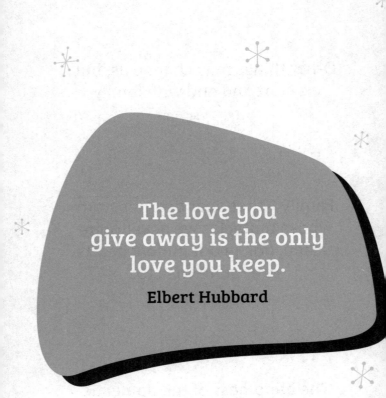

The love you
give away is the only
love you keep.

Elbert Hubbard

LIL'
DARLINGS

Children are the living messages
we send to a time we will not see.

NEIL POSTMAN

Grandparents, like heroes,
are as necessary to a child's
growth as vitamins.

JOYCE ALLSTON

Grandchildren don't
stay young forever, which is
good because Pop-pops have only
so many horsey rides in them.

GENE PERRET

THERE'S NOTHING THAT CAN HELP YOU UNDERSTAND YOUR BELIEFS MORE THAN TRYING TO EXPLAIN THEM TO AN INQUISITIVE CHILD.

Frank A. Clark

All children are artists.
The problem is how to remain
an artist once he grows up.

PABLO PICASSO

GRANDCHILDREN ARE THEIR GRANDPARENTS' TOYS.

Mokokoma Mokhonoana

To show a child what has
once delighted you, to find
the child's delight added to
your own… is happiness.

J. B. PRIESTLEY

Children have never been very good
at listening to their elders, but they
have never failed to imitate them.

JAMES A. BALDWIN

My granddaughter said…
'Granddad, were you in the Ark?'
'Of course not!' I replied. 'Then
why weren't you drowned?'

JAMES POTTER

The grandchildren should not bear
the debts of the grandparents.

NASSIM NICHOLAS TALEB

Children are unpredictable.
You never know what inconsistency
they're going to catch you in next.

FRANKLIN P. JONES

Like stars are to the sky, so
are the children to our world.
They deserve to shine!

CHINONYE J. CHIDOLUE

In order not to influence a child,
one must be careful not to be that
child's parent or grandparent.

DON MARQUIS

What is a home
without children?
Quiet.

HENNY YOUNGMAN

Children find everything in nothing;
men find nothing in everything.

GIACOMO LEOPARDI

No matter how many grandchildren
you may have, each one holds
a special place in your heart.

ALVARETTA ROBERTS

There never was a child so
lovely but his mother was
glad to get him asleep.

RALPH WALDO EMERSON

Those things your kids did that got
on your nerves seem so cute when
your grandchildren do them.

RAYMOND HOLLAND

CROWNED IN SILVER

By common consent grey hairs are a crown of glory; the only object of respect that can never excite envy.

GEORGE BANCROFT

Grey hair is the glory of a long life.

LAILAH GIFTY AKITA

Let us respect grey hairs, especially our own.

J. P. SEARS

[The] three stages
of man: he believes in
Santa Claus; he does not
believe in Santa Claus;
he is Santa Claus.

Bob Phillips

One thing to be said for wrinkles –
at least they don't hurt.

BETTY SMITH

White hairs are the crests of foam
which cover the sea after the tempest.

CARMEN SYLVA

Among all the fissures of his
wrinkles, there shone certain mild
gleams of a newly developing bloom
– the spring verdure peeping forth
even beneath February's snow.

HERMAN MELVILLE

His head was silver'd
o'er with age,
And long experience
made him sage.

JOHN GAY

BEAUTY AND UGLINESS
DISAPPEAR EQUALLY UNDER THE
WRINKLES OF AGE; ONE IS LOST IN
THEM; THE OTHER HIDDEN.

Jean Antoine Petit-Senn

THE BEST MIRROR IS AN OLD FRIEND.

George Herbert

No beauty is lost. You get to see the real face of it after the blossoms have fallen off the tree.

HENRY ROLLINS

AFTER A CERTAIN NUMBER
OF YEARS, OUR FACES BECOME
OUR BIOGRAPHIES.

Cynthia Ozick

White hair reminds you that time
has finally caught up with you.

BANGAMBIKI HABYARIMANA

An old man looks permanent, as if
he had always been an old man.

H. E. BATES

Grey hairs seem to my fancy
like the soft light of the moon,
silvering over the evening of life.

JEAN PAUL RICHTER

PERSISTENT SMILE BRINGS OUT HOLLOW DIMPLES, AND PERSISTENT FROWNS BRINGS OUT HOLLOW WRINKLES.

Michael Bassey Johnson

The discovery of a grey hair
when you are brushing out your
whiskers of a morning – first
fallen flake of the coming snows
of age – is a disagreeable thing.

ALEXANDER SMITH

Cheerfulness and contentment are
great beautifiers, and are fatuous
preservers of youthful looks.

CHARLES DICKENS

There is only one cure for grey hair.
It was invented by a Frenchman.
It is called the guillotine.

P. G. WODEHOUSE

GRANDPA KNOWS BEST

Wise words are like seeds.
The more you scatter them, the
more they will grow into infinite
gardens of knowledge.

SUZY KASSEM

A positive attitude may not
solve all your problems, but it
will annoy people enough to
make it worth the effort.

HERM ALBRIGHT

If you wait,
all that happens
is that you get older.

MARIO ANDRETTI

I've learned that making a 'living' is not the same thing as making a 'life'.

Maya Angelou

The life of every man is a diary
in which he means to write one
story, and writes another.

J. M. BARRIE

You must have control of the
authorship of your own destiny.

IRENE C. KASSORLA

The aim of life is to live, and to
live means to be aware, joyously,
drunkenly, serenely, divinely aware.

HENRY MILLER

Live as if you were to die tomorrow.
Learn as if you were to live forever.

MAHATMA GANDHI

It takes courage to grow up and
become who you really are.

E. E. CUMMINGS

You live and learn.
At any rate, you live.

DOUGLAS ADAMS

When any fit of gloominess, or perversion of mind, lays hold upon you, make it a rule not to publish it by complaints.

SAMUEL JOHNSON

FIND AN AIM IN LIFE BEFORE YOU RUN OUT OF AMMUNITION.

Arnold H. Glasow

HE WHO HAS A WHY TO LIVE CAN BEAR ALMOST ANY HOW.

Friedrich Nietzsche

If there be a hell upon earth, it is to be found in a melancholy man's heart.

ROBERT BURTON

The circumstances of the world are so variable that an irrevocable purpose or opinion is almost synonymous with a foolish one.

WILLIAM H. SEWARD

A diplomat is a man who always remembers a woman's birthday but never remembers her age.

ROBERT FROST

One's first step in wisdom
is to question everything –
and one's last is to come to
terms with everything.

GEORG CHRISTOPH LICHTENBERG

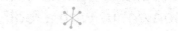

THE DIGNITY OF MAN LIES IN HIS ABILITY TO FACE REALITY IN ALL ITS MEANINGLESSNESS.

Martin Esslin

He who trims himself to suit everyone
will soon whittle himself away.

RAYMOND HULL

Life is a shipwreck but we must
not forget to sing in the lifeboats.

VOLTAIRE

Maybe all one can do is hope to
end up with the right regrets.

ARTHUR MILLER

FEELING CREAKY

The brain forgets much, but the lower back remembers everything.

ROBERT BRAULT

Old Age… when you stop taking drugs for fun and start taking them to keep you alive.

J. MATTHEW NESPOLI

People say that age is just a state of mind. I say it's more about the state of your body.

GEOFFREY PARFITT

THE OLDER I GROW THE MORE I DISTRUST THE FAMILIAR DOCTRINE THAT AGE BRINGS WISDOM.

H. L. Mencken

Old age puts more wrinkles in our minds than on our faces.

MICHEL DE MONTAIGNE

WHY IS IT THAT OUR MEMORY IS GOOD ENOUGH TO RETAIN THE LEAST TRIVIALITY THAT HAPPENS TO US, AND YET NOT GOOD ENOUGH TO RECOLLECT HOW OFTEN WE HAVE TOLD IT TO THE SAME PERSON?

François de La Rochefoucauld

As we grow older, our bodies get shorter and our anecdotes longer.

ROBERT QUILLEN

By the time you're eighty years old you've learned everything. You only have to remember it.

GEORGE BURNS

Life is one long process of getting tired.

SAMUEL BUTLER

Growing old isn't so bad when
you consider the alternative!

MAURICE CHEVALIER

GROWING OLD IS SOMETHING
YOU DO IF YOU'RE LUCKY.

Groucho Marx

The awful thing about getting old is that you have breakfast every half-hour.

Noël Coward

The excesses of our youth are drafts
upon our old age, payable with
interest about thirty years after date.

CHARLES CALEB COLTON

It has done me good
to be somewhat parched
by the heat and drenched
by the rain of life.

HENRY WADSWORTH LONGFELLOW

I've often thought that the
ageing process could be slowed
down if it had to work its way
through Parliament.

EDWINA CURRIE

He seems
To have seen better days,
as who has not
Who has seen yesterday?

LORD BYRON

There is only one difference between
a long life and a good dinner: that,
in the dinner, the sweets come last.

ROBERT LOUIS STEVENSON

I am a little deaf, a little blind, a little
impotent, and on top of this are two
or three abominable infirmities,
but nothing destroys my hope.

VOLTAIRE

THE
GOLDEN
YEARS

With mirth and laughter
let old wrinkles come.

WILLIAM SHAKESPEARE

Nothing is more enjoyable
than a leisured old age.

CICERO

No one can avoid ageing, but ageing
productively is something else.

KATHARINE GRAHAM

A HEALTHY OLD FELLOW, THAT IS NOT A FOOL, IS THE HAPPIEST CREATURE LIVING.

Richard Steele

Old age takes from the man of intellect no qualities save those that are useless to wisdom.

JOSEPH JOUBERT

Ageing seems to be the only available way to live a long life.

DANIEL FRANÇOIS ESPRIT AUBER

Cherish all your happy moments: they make a fine cushion for old age.

CHRISTOPHER MORLEY

It is gracious to have old people
full of vitality and endowed
with wisdom in our society.

LAILAH GIFTY AKITA

Life is most delightful when it is on
the downward slope, but has not
yet reached the abrupt decline.

SENECA

We turn not older with years,
but newer every day.

EMILY DICKINSON

OLD WOOD BEST TO BURN, OLD WINE TO DRINK, OLD FRIENDS TO TRUST, AND OLD AUTHORS TO READ.

Francis Bacon

How blest is he who crowns,
in shades like these,
A youth of labour with an age of ease!

OLIVER GOLDSMITH

The evening of a well-spent life
brings its lamps with it.

JOSEPH JOUBERT

Age, toward which you draw amid
the storms of life, is nothing so
dreadful. Those who call it so have
found all stages of life unwelcome,
thanks to their mishandling of
life, not to a particular age.

FRANCESCO PETRARCH

You can't turn back the clock.
But you can wind it up again.

BONNIE PRUDDEN

As we grow old we become
more foolish and more wise.

FRANÇOIS DE LA ROCHEFOUCAULD

You get old and you realize there
are no answers, just stories.

GARRISON KEILLOR

The secret of genius is to carry the
spirit of the child into old age, which
means never losing your enthusiasm.

ALDOUS HUXLEY

We look forward to a
disreputable, vigorous, unhonoured
and disorderly old age.

DON MARQUIS

Men, like peaches and pears,
grow sweet a little while before
they begin to decay.

OLIVER WENDELL HOLMES JR

A WRINKLE
IN TIME

The whiter my hair becomes,
the more ready people are
to believe what I say.

BERTRAND RUSSELL

Whenever a man's friends begin
to compliment him about looking
young, he may be sure that
they think he is growing old.

WASHINGTON IRVING

Even young grandparents
seem enormously old to a
small child, although the child
may politely deny it.

ALISON JUDSON RYERSON

Wrinkles should merely indicate where smiles have been.

Mark Twain

You can't help getting older, but
you don't have to get old.

GEORGE BURNS

AGE IS FREQUENTLY
BEAUTIFUL, WISDOM APPEARING
LIKE AN AFTERMATH.

Benjamin Disraeli

A person is always startled when
he hears himself seriously called
an old man for the first time.

OLIVER WENDELL HOLMES JR

[Old age is] the most unexpected of
all things that happen to a man.

LEON TROTSKY

The satirical rogue says here, that
old men have grey beards; that
their faces are wrinkled; … and that
they have a plentiful lack of wit.

WILLIAM SHAKESPEARE

You know you're getting old
when all the names in your black
book have MD after them.

ARNOLD PALMER

Time, which changes people,
does not alter the image we
have retained of them.

MARCEL PROUST

We advance in years somewhat in the
manner of an invading army in a barren
land; the age that we have reached,
as the saying goes, we but hold
with an outpost, and still keep open
communications with the extreme rear
and first beginnings of the march.

ROBERT LOUIS STEVENSON

Every wrinkle [is] but a notch in the quiet calendar of a well-spent life.

CHARLES DICKENS

Men blossomed in a kind of autumnal youth, they seemed more dignified with their first grey hairs.

GABRIEL GARCÍA MÁRQUEZ

Autumn carries more gold in its pocket than all the other seasons.

JIM BISHOP

IN OLD AGE YOU MUST PUT UP WITH THE FACE, THE FRIENDS, THE HEALTH, AND THE CHILDREN YOU HAVE EARNED.

Fay Weldon

HAIRY
MOMENTS

Better a bald head than none at all.
AUSTIN O'MALLEY

The tenderest spot in a man's
make-up is sometimes the bald
spot on top of his head.
HELEN ROWLAND

I used to think I'd like less grey hair.
Now I think I'd like more of it.
RICHIE BENAUD

THERE IS MORE FELICITY ON THE FAR SIDE OF BALDNESS THAN YOUNG MEN CAN POSSIBLY IMAGINE.

Logan Pearsall Smith

It seems no more than right that men
should seize time by the forelock,
for the rude old fellow, sooner or
later, pulls all their hair out.

GEORGE DENNISON PRENTICE

Bald as the bare mountain tops are
bald, with a baldness full of grandeur.

MATTHEW ARNOLD

Hair loss is God's way of
telling me I'm human.

BRUCE WILLIS

We lose our hair, our teeth!
Our bloom, our ideals.

SAMUEL BECKETT

THERE'S ONE THING ABOUT BALDNESS; IT'S NEAT.

Don Herold

I knew I was going bald when it was taking longer and longer to wash my face.

Harry Hill

Anyone can be confident with a full head of hair. But a confident bald man – there's your diamond in the rough.

LARRY DAVID

A MAN IS USUALLY BALD FOUR OR FIVE YEARS BEFORE HE KNOWS IT.

Ed Howe

A hair in the head is worth
two in the brush.

OLIVER HERFORD

There is nothing more
contemptible than a bald man
who pretends to have hair.

MARCUS VALERIUS MARTIAL

We will not tolerate any
familiarity with the toupee
which covers our baldness.

ERIC HOFFER

I was going to buy a book on hair loss, but the pages kept falling out.

JAY LONDON

EXPERIENCE IS A COMB WHICH NATURE GIVES TO MEN WHEN THEY ARE BALD.

Chinese proverb

I like to play chess with
bald men in the park although
it's hard to find 32 of them.

EMO PHILIPS

I love bald men. Just
because you've lost your fuzz
don't mean you ain't a peach.

DOLLY PARTON

I'd rather be bald on
top than bald inside.

JOE GARAGIOLA

YOUNG AT HEART

You are only young once, but you
can stay immature indefinitely.

OGDEN NASH

Growing old is no more than
a bad habit which a busy
man has no time to form.

ANDRÉ MAUROIS

I'm saving that rocker for the day
when I feel as old as I really am.

DWIGHT D. EISENHOWER

THE AGEING PROCESS HAS YOU FIRMLY IN ITS GRASP IF YOU NEVER GET THE URGE TO THROW A SNOWBALL.

Doug Larson

Age is a very high price to
pay for maturity.
TOM STOPPARD

Youth would be an ideal state
if it came a little later in life.
H. H. ASQUITH

Inside every older person is a younger
person wondering what happened.
JENNIFER YANE

Age makes us not childish, as some say; it finds us still true children.

JOHANN WOLFGANG VON GOETHE

The great secret that all old people share is that you really haven't changed in seventy or eighty years.

DORIS LESSING

It is not by the grey of the hair that one knows the age of the heart.

EDWARD BULWER-LYTTON

It is the rudest word in my dictionary, 'retire'. And 'old' is another one… I like 'enthusiastic'.

JUDI DENCH

THE TRUE WAY TO RENDER AGE VIGOROUS IS TO PROLONG THE YOUTH OF THE MIND.

Mortimer Collins

A PRUNE IS AN EXPERIENCED PLUM.

John Trather

The mind of man, his brain,
and nerves, are a truer index of
his age than the calendar.

PERCY BYSSHE SHELLEY

If wrinkles must be written
upon our brows, let them not
be written upon the heart. The
spirit should not grow old.

JAMES A. GARFIELD

May we keep a little of the fuel of
youth to warm our body in old age.

MINNA THOMAS ANTRIM

The idea is to die young as late as possible.

ASHLEY MONTAGU

None are so old as those who have outlived enthusiasm.

HENRY DAVID THOREAU

I was wise enough to never grow up while fooling most people into believing I had.

MARGARET MEAD

STILL
GOT IT!

You still chase women,
but only downhill.

Old is when your wife says, 'Let's go
upstairs and make love,' and you
answer, 'Honey, I can't do both.'

RED BUTTONS

You're getting old when a four-letter
word for something pleasurable two
people can do in bed is R-E-A-D.

DENIS NORDEN

The older one grows, the more one likes indecency.

Virginia Woolf

As you get older, the pickings get slimmer, but the people don't.

CARRIE FISHER

Nothing makes people crosser than being considered too old for love.

NANCY MITFORD

In youth we are plagued by desire; in later years, by the desire to feel desire.

MIGNON McLAUGHLIN

A man can be short and dumpy
and getting bald but if he has
fire, women will like him.

MAE WEST

Don't worry about avoiding
temptation – as you grow older,
it starts avoiding you.

MICHAEL FORD

Those who love deeply
never grow old; they may die of
old age, but they die young.

ARTHUR W. PINERO

An inordinate passion for pleasure
is the secret of remaining young.

OSCAR WILDE

If youth only knew
and age only could.

ROBERT LOUIS STEVENSON

Age does not protect you from
love. But love, to some extent,
protects you from age.

JEANNE MOREAU

To see an old couple loving each other is the best sight of all.

WILLIAM MAKEPEACE THACKERAY

YOU KNOW YOU ARE GETTING OLD WHEN YOUR IDEA OF HOT, FLAMING DESIRE IS A BARBECUED STEAK.

Victoria Fabiano

OLD AGE LIKES INDECENCY. IT'S A SIGN OF LIFE.

Mason Cooley

A man is not old as long
as he is seeking something.

JEAN ROSTAND

WHEN DID MY WILD OATS TURN TO PRUNES AND ALL-BRAN?

Lucy Parker

A TINKER
AND A
POTTER

I am getting to an age when I can
only enjoy the last sport left. It is
called hunting for your spectacles.

EDWARD GREY

Preserving tradition has become a
nice hobby, like stamp collecting.

MASON COOLEY

I am not against golf, since I cannot
but suspect it keeps armies of the
unworthy from discovering trout.

PAUL O'NEILL

A HOBBY A DAY KEEPS
THE DOLDRUMS AWAY.

Phyllis McGinley

The gods do not deduct
from man's allotted span the
hours spent in fishing.

BABYLONIAN PROVERB

Retirement kills more people
than hard work ever did.

MALCOLM FORBES

There is certainly something in
angling that tends to produce
a serenity of the mind.

WASHINGTON IRVING

Fishing is much more than fish. It is the great occasion when we may return to the… simplicity of our forefathers.

HERBERT HOOVER

Golf is a game that needlessly prolongs the lives of some of our most useless citizens.

BOB HOPE

Life is more fun if you play games.

ROALD DAHL

We don't stop playing because we grow old; we grow old because we stop playing.

G. Stanley Hall

Golf is a day spent in a round
of strenuous idleness.

WILLIAM WORDSWORTH

I regard golf as an expensive
way of playing marbles.

GILBERT K. CHESTERTON

Golf is played by twenty million
mature American men whose wives
think they are out having fun.

JIM BISHOP

Don't simply retire *from* something;
have something to retire *to*.

HARRY EMERSON FOSDICK

I don't think I can be expected
to take seriously any game which
takes less than three days to
reach its conclusion.

TOM STOPPARD

If a man watches three
football games in a row, he should
be declared legally dead.

ERMA BOMBECK

The worst time to have
a heart attack is during a
game of charades.

DEMETRI MARTIN

THE ELDERLY DON'T DRIVE THAT
BADLY; THEY'RE JUST THE ONLY ONES
WITH TIME TO DO THE SPEED LIMIT.

Jason Love

RETIREMENT IS WONDERFUL. IT'S DOING NOTHING WITHOUT WORRYING ABOUT GETTING CAUGHT AT IT.

Gene Perret

GRANDBAR

Beer is proof God loves us and
wants us to be happy.

BENJAMIN FRANKLIN

Jameson's Irish Whiskey
really does improve with age:
the older I get the more I like it.

BOB MONKHOUSE

The secret to a long life is…
don't drink too much. Then
again, don't drink too little.

HERMAN SMITH-JOHANNSEN

MODERATION IS THE KEY TO OLD AGE AND THE DOORWAY TO BOREDOM.

Benny Bellamacina

Alcohol is the anaesthesia by which
we endure the operation of life.

GEORGE BERNARD SHAW

Is not old wine wholesomest…?

JOHN WEBSTER

The vine produces more grapes
when it is young, but better grapes
for wine when it is old, because its
juices are more perfectly concocted.

FRANCIS BACON

The last drink delights the toper, the glass which souses him and puts the finishing touch on his drunkenness.

SENECA

DON'T TRUST A BRILLIANT IDEA UNLESS IT SURVIVES THE HANGOVER.

Jimmy Breslin

I envy people who drink – at least they know what to blame everything on.

Oscar Levant

I don't have a beer belly.
It's a Burgundy belly and it cost
me a lot of money.

CHARLES CLARKE

Fleeting is every earthly joy,
Wait not till time its bloom destroy,
But pluck the rose, nor pause to think,
But drink!

THEODOR KÖRNER

I feel sorry for people who don't
drink. When they wake up in
the morning, that's as good as
they're going to feel all day.

FRANK SINATRA

ALCOHOL IS A MISUNDERSTOOD VITAMIN.

P. G. Wodehouse

Health – what my friends are always
drinking to before they fall down.

PHYLLIS DILLER

Almost anything can be
preserved in alcohol, except
health, happiness, and money.

MARY WILSON LITTLE

If I had my life to live over,
I'd live over a saloon.

W. C. FIELDS

I have taken more out of alcohol
than alcohol has taken out of me.

WINSTON CHURCHILL

Age still leaves us friends and wine.

THOMAS MOORE

Drink to-day, and drown all sorrow;
You shall perhaps not do it to-morrow:
Best, while you have it, use your breath;
There is no drinking after death.

FRANCIS BEAUMONT AND JOHN FLETCHER

GRANDAD'S
GARDEN

But tho' an old man, I am
but a young gardener.

THOMAS JEFFERSON

WHENEVER YOU ARE CREATING
BEAUTY AROUND YOU, YOU ARE
RESTORING YOUR OWN SOUL.

Alice Walker

IF YOU PLANT A WALNUT YOU ARE PLANTING IT FOR YOUR GRANDCHILDREN.

George Orwell

Gardening… does not allow
one to be mentally old, because
too many hopes and dreams are
yet to be realised.

ALLAN ARMITAGE

Old gardeners never die.
They just spade away and then
throw in the trowel.

HERBERT V. PROCHNOW

If you have a garden and a library,
you have everything you need.

CICERO

Young twigs will bend
but not old trees.

DUTCH PROVERB

GARDENING REQUIRES LOTS OF
WATER — MOST OF IT IN THE
FORM OF PERSPIRATION.

Lou Erickson

Gardens are a form of autobiography.

Sydney Eddison

My garden now grows hope in lavish profusion, leaving little room for anything else.

SHARON KAY PENMAN

To forget how to dig the earth and to tend the soil is to forget ourselves.

MAHATMA GANDHI

The soil is the great connector of our lives, the source and destination of all.

WENDELL BERRY

The garden is about life and
beauty and the impermanence of
all living things.

ANNE LAMOTT

To plant a garden is to
believe in tomorrow.

AUDREY HEPBURN

If you need five tools to solve
a problem in the garden, four
of them will be easy to find.

MIKE GAROFALO

Nothing is more completely the
child of art than a garden.

WALTER SCOTT

Garden as though you
will live forever.

WILLIAM KENT

A garden is a love song, a
duet between a human being
and Mother Nature.

JEFF COX

A garden is always a series
of losses set against a few
triumphs, like life itself.

MAY SARTON

There is no gardening without
humility. Nature is constantly
sending even its oldest scholars
to the bottom of the class for
some egregious blunder.

ALFRED AUSTIN

The philosopher who said that
work well done never needs doing
over never weeded a garden.

RAY D. EVERSON

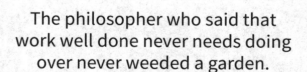

THE GOOD
OLD DAYS

My grandfather always said that living
is like licking honey off a thorn.

LOUIS ADAMIC

My grandfather tell me
not to hold the knowledge
to myself; I have to pass it on.

MAU PIAILUG

I think I don't regret a single 'excess'
of my responsive youth – I only regret,
in my chilled age, certain occasions
and possibilities I didn't embrace.

HENRY JAMES

NOSTALGIA IS A FILE THAT REMOVES THE ROUGH EDGES FROM THE GOOD OLD DAYS.

Doug Larson

Nostalgia, the vice of the aged.
ANGELA CARTER

Nothing is more responsible for the good old days than a bad memory.
FRANKLIN P. ADAMS

More and more, when I single out the person who inspired me most, I go back to my grandfather.
JAMES EARL JONES

The passionate commitment I have to bringing people together without regard to race, it all started with my grandfather.

BILL CLINTON

MY GRANDFATHER WAS THE MOST SELFLESS PERSON I KNOW.

Cat Dugdale

WE GROW GREY IN OUR SPIRIT LONG BEFORE WE GROW GREY IN OUR HAIR.

Charles Lamb

Our Spring and our Summer are
gone by, and they will never be seen
on earth again save in memory.

J. R. R. TOLKIEN

Sweet childish days, that were as long
As twenty days are now.

WILLIAM WORDSWORTH

It well becomes a man
who is no longer young to
forget that he ever was.

SEIGNEUR DE SAINT-ÉVREMOND

My Hungarian grandfather was
the kind of man that could follow
someone into a revolving door
and come out first.

STEPHEN FRY

HOME IS A PLACE YOU GROW UP
WANTING TO LEAVE, AND GROW OLD
WANTING TO GET BACK TO.

John Ed Pearce

My grandfather was a giant of a man...
When he walked, the earth shook.

ETH CLIFFORD

A man is not old until regrets
take the place of dreams.

JOHN BARRYMORE

My grandfather was a wonderful
role model. Through him I got to
know the gentle side of men.

SARAH LONG

It is, I suppose, the business of grandparents to create memories and the relative of memories: traditions.

ELLEN GOODMAN

PLEASURE IS THE FLOWER THAT PASSES; REMEMBRANCE, THE LASTING PERFUME.

Jean de Boufflers

WISDOM OF THE AGED

Old men are fond of giving good advice, to console themselves for being no longer in a position to give bad examples.

FRANÇOIS DE LA ROCHEFOUCAULD

THE IMPORTANT THING... IS NOT HOW MANY YEARS IN YOUR LIFE, BUT HOW MUCH LIFE IN YOUR YEARS!

Edward J. Stieglitz

Retire from work,
but not from life.

M. K. Soni

In an aged man appears ripeness
of wisdom: in an old sandal-tree
is produced the fragrance.

SATAKA, HINDU WISDOM

Life is the sum of all your choices.

ALBERT CAMUS

No wise man ever wished
to be younger.

JONATHAN SWIFT

To know how to grow old is the master-work of wisdom, and one of the most difficult chapters in the great art of living.

HENRI-FRÉDÉRIC AMIEL

AS I GROW OLDER, I PAY LESS ATTENTION TO WHAT MEN SAY. I JUST WATCH WHAT THEY DO.

Andrew Carnegie

Age is only a number, a cipher for
the records. A man can't retire
his experience. He must use it.

BERNARD BARUCH

My son, we ought to lay up a stock
of absurd enthusiasms in our youth,
or else we shall reach the end of our
journey with an empty heart, for
we lose a great many on our way.

VICTOR CHERBULIEZ

Wisdom doesn't necessarily
come with age. Sometimes age
just shows up all by itself.

TOM WILSON

THE GREATEST TRICK YOU CAN TEACH AN OLD DOG IS HOW TO LEARN NEW TRICKS.

J. S. Davey

Man often acquires just so much
knowledge as to discover his
ignorance, and attains so much
experience as to see and regret
his follies, and then dies.

WILLIAM BENTON CLULOW

We age inevitably:
The old joys fade and are gone:
And at last comes equanimity and
the flame burning clear.

JAMES OPPENHEIM

Life is a country that the old have
seen, and lived in. Those who have
to travel through it can only learn
the way from them.

JOSEPH JOUBERT

The art of life is the art
of avoiding pain.

THOMAS JEFFERSON

Superfluity comes sooner by white
hairs, but competency lives longer.

WILLIAM SHAKESPEARE

Perhaps nothing 'ud be a lesson
if it didn't come too late.

GEORGE ELIOT

Life is a long road on
a short journey.

JAMES LENDALL BASFORD

THE YOUNG SOW WILD OATS,
THE OLD GROW SAGE.

Henry James Byron

MEMENTO MORI

Gather ye rosebuds while ye may,
Old Time is still a-flying;
And this same flower that smiles today
Tomorrow will be dying.

ROBERT HERRICK

As you grow older, you'll find the
only things you regret are the
things you didn't do.

ZACHARY SCOTT

The most positive way to think
about death is to try to live.

MICHAEL CAINE

AGE, THAT LESSENS THE ENJOYMENT OF LIFE, INCREASES OUR DESIRE OF LIVING.

Oliver Goldsmith

Your time is limited, so don't
waste it living someone else's life.

STEVE JOBS

I AM NOW OLD ENOUGH
TO NO LONGER HAVE A
FEAR OF DYING YOUNG.

Bruce Ades

I want to die young
at an advanced age.

MAX LERNER

LIFE WAS A FUNNY THING THAT HAPPENED TO ME ON THE WAY TO THE GRAVE.

Quentin Crisp

LIFE DOES NOT CEASE TO BE FUNNY WHEN PEOPLE DIE ANY MORE THAN IT CEASES TO BE SERIOUS WHEN PEOPLE LAUGH.

George Bernard Shaw

Life is pleasant. Death is peaceful. It's the transition that's troublesome.

ISAAC ASIMOV

I am prepared to meet my Maker. Whether my Maker is prepared for the ordeal of meeting me is another matter.

WINSTON CHURCHILL

Memorial services are the cocktail parties of the geriatric set.

HAROLD MACMILLAN

I know of nothing
more laughable than
a doctor who does not
die of old age.

VOLTAIRE

WHENEVER I GET DOWN ABOUT
LIFE GOING BY TOO QUICKLY, WHAT
HELPS ME IS A LITTLE MANTRA THAT
I REPEAT TO MYSELF: AT LEAST
I'M NOT A FRUIT FLY.

Ray Romano

Death twitches my ear.
'Live,' he says, 'I am coming.'

VIRGIL

Old age is like waiting in the
departure lounge of life. Fortunately,
we are in England and the
train is bound to be late.

MILTON SHULMAN

Wisdom comes to us when it can
no longer do any good.

GABRIEL GARCÍA MÁRQUEZ

Our bodies are the burial grounds of dead time.

T. A. SACHS

As a well-spent day brings happy sleep, so a life well used brings happy death.

LEONARDO DA VINCI

I shall not die of a cold… I shall die of having lived.

WILLA CATHER

Death is not the end. There remains the litigation over the estate.

Ambrose Bierce

IT WASN'T LIKE THAT IN MY DAY...

Lately I sometimes ask myself how many more new tricks I *want* to learn.

RAM DASS

The one time I did get the computer on, I couldn't turn the damn thing off!

WILLIAM SHATNER

It now costs more to amuse a child than it once did to educate his father.

VAUGHN MONROE

In the old days, people robbed stagecoaches and knocked off armoured trucks. Now they're knocking off servers.

RICHARD POWER

WE LIVE IN AN AGE WHEN PIZZA GETS TO YOUR HOME BEFORE THE POLICE.

Jeff Marder

I don't answer the phone. I get the feeling whenever I do that there will be someone on the other end.

FRED COUPLES

As lousy as things are now, tomorrow they will be somebody's good old days.

GERALD BARZAN

HE THAT WILL NOT APPLY NEW REMEDIES MUST EXPECT NEW EVILS; FOR TIME IS THE GREATEST INNOVATOR.

Francis Bacon

It is the nature of a man as he grows older… to protest against change.

JOHN STEINBECK

I go to my grandchildren. They keep their grandpa informed on what's going on.

BEN VEREEN

It was not so long ago that people thought… microchips were very, very small snack foods.

GERALDINE FERRARO

The days of the digital
watch are numbered.

TOM STOPPARD

THE MOST OVERLOOKED ADVANTAGE TO OWNING A COMPUTER IS THAT IF THEY FOUL UP, THERE'S NO LAW AGAINST WHACKING THEM AROUND.

Eric Porterfield

I never expected to see the day when girls would get sunburned in the places they do now.

WILL ROGERS

THE PEOPLE WHO LIVE IN A GOLDEN AGE USUALLY GO AROUND COMPLAINING HOW YELLOW EVERYTHING LOOKS.

Randall Jarrell

Life has no auto-settings. No
batteries. You gots to wind it up!

JEB DICKERSON

Every man desires to live long,
but no man would be old.

JONATHAN SWIFT

In spite of the cost of living,
it's still popular.

KATHLEEN NORRIS

YOUTH OF
TODAY

Your modern teenager is
not about to listen to advice
from an old person.

DAVE BARRY

THERE IS NOTHING WRONG WITH
THE YOUNGER GENERATION WHICH
THE OLDER GENERATION DID
NOT OUTGROW.

Anonymous

I didn't turn into...
a grumpy old man.
I was a grumpy
teenager as well.

Rory McGrath

Kids today never say, 'Man, I'm really into remote-controlled steamboats.'

JACK WHITE

Youth is the most beautiful thing in this world… what a pity that it has to be wasted on children!

GEORGE BERNARD SHAW

The 'teenager' seems to have replaced the Communist as the appropriate target for public controversy and foreboding.

EDGAR Z. FRIEDENBERG

The denunciation of the young is a necessary part of the hygiene of older people, and greatly assists in the circulation of their blood.

LOGAN PEARSALL SMITH

The older generation thought nothing of getting up at five… and the younger generation doesn't think much of it either.

JOHN J. WELSH

Old ones should respect the energy of youths and youths should respect the experience of old ones.

AMIT KALANTRI

THERE WAS NO RESPECT FOR YOUTH WHEN I WAS YOUNG... NOW THAT I AM OLD, THERE IS NO RESPECT FOR AGE.

J. B. Priestley

Empathy is what separates human beings from teenage boys.

VICTOR LAVALLE

In youth men are apt to write more wisely than they really know or feel; and the remainder of life may be not idly spent in realizing and convincing themselves of the wisdom which they uttered long ago.

NATHANIEL HAWTHORNE

I despair of teaching anyone anything, least of all myself.

GORE VIDAL

To get back my youth I would do anything in the world, except take exercise, get up early, or be respectable.

OSCAR WILDE

If you want to recapture your youth, just cut off his allowance.

AL BERNSTEIN

Live as long as you may, the first twenty years are the longest half of your life.

ROBERT SOUTHEY

Teenagers complain there's nothing
to do, then stay out all night doing it.

BOB PHILLIPS

One thing only has been lent
To youth and age in
common – discontent.

MATTHEW ARNOLD

It is better to waste one's youth
than to do nothing with it at all.

GEORGES COURTELINE

GRANDPA
IS THE
BEST!

Grandfather is the wisest person
in the house but few of the
household listen.

CHINESE PROVERB

With your grandparents you
have a feeling that you can say
anything or you can do anything,
and they will support you.

NOVAK DJOKOVIC

Few things are more delightful than
grandchildren fighting over your lap.

DOUG LARSON

A FAMILY WITH AN OLD PERSON HAS A LIVING TREASURE OF GOLD.

Chinese proverb

I have kept my good humour and take neither myself nor the next person seriously.

ALBERT EINSTEIN

OUR FACES WILL BECOME WORKS OF ART THAT OUR GRANDCHILDREN WILL TREASURE.

Adriana Trigiani

It is so comic to hear oneself called old, even at ninety, I suppose!

ALICE JAMES

I didn't get old on purpose, it just happened. If you're lucky, it could happen to you.

ANDY ROONEY

You make all your mistakes with your own children, so by the time your grandchildren arrive, you… get it right.

LIZ FENTON

Every generation
revolts against its fathers
and makes friends with
its grandfathers.

Lewis Mumford

Grandfather knows that after the fun and games are over with his adorable grandchildren he can return to… his own home.

ALVIN F. POUSSAINT

Young people must appreciate the beauty of old age. The old people were once young.

LAILAH GIFTY AKITA

One of life's greatest mysteries
is how the boy who wasn't good
enough to marry your daughter can
be the father of the smartest
grandchild in the world.

JEWISH PROVERB

What a bargain grandchildren are!
I give them my loose change, and
they give me a million dollars'
worth of pleasure.

GENE PERRET

I have never once regretted
missing a business opportunity
so that I could be with my
children and grandchildren.

MITT ROMNEY

HOLDING A GREAT-GRANDCHILD MAKES GETTING OLD WORTHWHILE.

Evalyn Rikkers

GRANDMA'S
WIT AND WISDOM

QUIPS AND QUOTES FOR THE GREATEST GRANNIES

RICHARD BENSON

GRANDMA'S WIT AND WISDOM
Quips and Quotes for the Greatest Grannies

Richard Benson

ISBN: 978-1-78685-063-8

Hardback
£9.99

When there are sticky handprints on the sofa and you can't prise the darlings away from a screen, reach into your handbag for this hilarious book, crammed full of quips and quotes to remind you why being a grandma is one of the best jobs in the world.

'Most grandmas have a touch of the scallywag.'
HELEN THOMSON

OLD GIT
WIT AND WISDOM

QUIPS AND QUOTES FOR THE YOUNG AT HEART

RICHARD BENSON

OLD GIT WIT AND WISDOM
Quips and Quotes for the Young at Heart

Richard Benson

ISBN: 978-1-78685-059-1

Hardback
£9.99

So you're getting on a bit, but even if your body creaks more than it used to, you've still got your sense of humour. This collection of witty quotations and gems of senior sagacity will keep a spring in your step and the cobwebs at bay.

'The older one grows, the more one likes indecency.'
VIRGINIA WOOLF

If you're interested in finding out more about our books, find us on Facebook at Summersdale Publishers and follow us on Twitter at @Summersdale.

www.summersdale.com